DD0409-NT

An Owl in the House

An Owl

in the House

A Naturalist's Diary

by Bernd Heinrich

Adapted by
Alice Calaprice

*With drawings and photographs
by the author*

LITTLE, BROWN AND COMPANY
Boston Toronto London

FIRST EDITION

This book is adapted from *One Man's Owl* by Bernd Heinrich. Copyright © 1987 by Princeton University Press. By permission of Princeton University Press.

The chapter "Baby Birds: The Problems" by Gale Lawrence is included by permission of the author. It is adapted from material appearing in *The Beginning Naturalist* by Gale Lawrence, published by The New England Press, Inc., Shelburne, Vermont.

Library of Congress Cataloging-in-Publication Data
Heinrich, Bernd, 1940–
    An owl in the house: a naturalist's diary / by Bernd Heinrich; adapted by Alice Calaprice; with drawings and photographs by the author.
       p.   cm.
    Summary: A field journal tracking the development of a great horned owlet, rescued in the wild, as it grows into an independent hunter able to survive in its own habitat.
    Bibliography: p.
    ISBN 0-316-35456-2
    1. Horned owl — Juvenile literature. 2. Wildlife rescue — Juvenile literature. [1. Horned owl. 2. Owls. 3. Wildlife rescue.] I. Calaprice, Alice. II. Title.
    QL696.S83H44 1990
    598'.97 — dc20   89-12473
                                                CIP
                                                AC

Joy Street Books are published by Little, Brown and Company (Inc.)

10 9 8 7 6 5 4 3 2 1

BP

Published simultaneously in Canada by Little, Brown & Company (Canada) Limited
PRINTED IN THE UNITED STATES OF AMERICA

To
Erica and Stuart
and
Denise and David

Contents

Preface

A few years ago I did something that I probably shouldn't have done, but to my mind I didn't have much of a choice, really. I adopted a wild animal — a baby great horned owl — after I found it buried in the snow in the Vermont woods near my home.

I am a zoologist and a naturalist. That means I study animals that live in the wild. I know very well that wild animals should usually be left to fend for themselves, and that many die an early death in the process. This is the way nature intended it to be. It is unkind to force a wild animal into captivity. Tampering with nature's ways causes the natural system of interdependence of all wild animals and plants to become unbalanced. In addition, most wild animals die when they leave their natural habitat and food supply. Despite this knowledge, I felt a moment of kinship with the owlet and instinctively reached out to protect it. I could not leave it there to die.

Most wild animals are protected by government agencies, and it is illegal to take them as pets. But I knew that, because I am a scientist, I could get permission to keep the owl and to study its development. I was very curious about how a docile owlet develops into a large and fierce predator; I was also curious about how this owl would interact with human beings.

Male and female owlets look alike, so for no particular reason I decided to refer to this one as "he." I named him Bubo, which is part of his scientific name, *Bubo virginianus*. Bubo became very special to me, and I think I was special to him.

I decided to keep a diary of Bubo's growth and development. Field biologists call such a diary a "field notebook"; in it they keep a record of their observations, speculate about what may be going on with the animal's behavior, and sometimes express their feelings at the moment of observation. I wanted to do all of that with Bubo. I knew I would have to teach him to fend for himself, but I had a hunch that he would have much more to teach me — about himself, about great horned owls in general, and probably even about myself.

Camp Kaflunk, Maine
November 1986

Wild Owls

By mid-March in northern Vermont, the snow from the winter storms is already beginning to thaw during the day, but the cold nights still produce a hard white crust on the ground. The warmer temperatures are beginning to trigger the flow of sap from the sugar maples, and you can feel that spring is just around the corner.

From where I stood at the edge of the thick woods overlooking Shelburne Bog, I felt a cold breeze pushing in from the north. Eerie creaking, scraping, and moaning sounds invaded the forest. The sky was turning dark, and the woods were growing pitch-black. Above the wind, I heard a booming, resonating "hoo-hoo-*hooo*-hoo!" To me it was a friendly sound, for I knew it was the call of a great horned owl.

When I returned to the same woods in early April, the signs of spring were more abundant. Some flowers were beginning to pop through the damp brown forest floor, birds were starting to build their nests, and the

The hemlock woods where Bubo was found

first spring peepers were calling out from the pond. In the dusk, I briefly saw a dark silhouette glide silently over the pines. I knew instantly that it was a large owl, maybe the one I had heard the month before. It vanished behind the pines, but not from my mind. I returned again on April 17, hoping to see the owl once more. And sure enough, through the thick evergreen branches I caught a glimpse of a large owl with ear tufts — a great horned owl. For a moment, our eyes met, and then the big bird turned its head and launched itself over the darkening forest.

Of all the owls, the great horned owl is the supreme predator. Among the predatory birds of North America, it is exceeded in weight only by eagles. This awesome bird has been called the "winged tiger"; but as I watched it glide quietly through the dusk, it did not seem savage at all.

I was curious to know if an owl's nest might be out there, so I set out to search for it before nightfall. I came across the nests of various birds, but one in particular caught my attention. I recognized the nest as a crow's nest, but that made no difference; great horned owls have never learned to build nests, so they use either large tree hollows or nests already built by crows, hawks, ravens, or other large birds. But crows, for instance, clean up the droppings of their young, and I noticed that whitewash splotched some of the branches. Then I noticed bird pellets on the forest floor. These

Owl pellets

are hard, dry, oval-shaped balls of fur, feathers, bones, and insect remains that owls (and some other birds) can't digest, so they cough them up, or "regurgitate" them. There is a mystery behind each pellet, and some people like to open them up to see what's inside. You can often tell what the bird ate, and from that you try to guess what kind of bird it may have been. If, for example, a pellet contains the remains of a rodent, it is probably an owl or hawk pellet. When I opened one of the pellets, I recognized the bones of a mouse. But the nest I saw could not have been used by a hawk because hawks do not have young so early in the season. I therefore concluded that these must be owl pellets. Furthermore, the owl was probably a great horned owl, because the other local woodland owls nest in hollow trees. In addition, I found feathers and bones in the area, which indicated to me that this was the nest of a powerful predator. I climbed high into a nearby pine tree so that I could look down inside the nest, and there they were — three fuzzy owlets inside their battered old home.

Great horned owl parents defend their nests fiercely, and it wasn't long before the mother owl came on the scene. She snapped her bill, called repeatedly in a hoarse gurgle, and occasionally hooted while staring at me with her huge yellow eyes. Her actions were meant to frighten me away, but she made no attempt to attack me. Being perched none too solidly on top of that large pine, I was grateful indeed that she didn't consider me a threat.

Two days later, the sky turned dark early in the day as storm clouds gathered from the north. The wind stopped blowing, and in the hushed silence, a sticky wet snow began to fall.

Despite the bad weather, I decided to return to the nest to see how the owlets were faring. I made my way through the forest, pulling my hat and scarf closer to my body as the wind delivered its chill. I arrived at the tree only to find that it was badly damaged from the storm. Tangles of branches lay beneath it in piles of soft snow. Two young owlets were perched safely on some fallen limbs. Where was the third?

I pulled out one branch, then another and another. I kicked some snow aside. Nothing. Then — what was

New owlet

that? A foot? No doubt about it — an owl's foot was sticking out of the snow! I gently brushed the powdery white stuff aside.

The owlet attached to that foot was too weak to stand. It was a soggy, sorry-looking little bundle. It lay on its side, head hunched down between its shoulders like a turtle in its shell. Its stubby wings moved weakly in slow motion, and its bill was partially open in fright as it stared up at me. Only the eyes showed some signs of life. I plucked up the limp little bird and carefully tucked it inside my jacket. I decided there was nothing to do but take it home.

Bubo as new-found owlet

An Owl in the House

April 21

Revived by the warmth of the wood-burning stove, Bubo stands up in his grass-filled cardboard box, glares at me, and hisses. I dangle a piece of meat in front of him, but he ignores it. As I gently push the meat inside his open bill, he at first remains motionless, then greedily swallows the morsel. Each succeeding piece of meat I offer goes down faster than the one before. As the nourishment revives him, all signs of shyness begin to fade.

Well fed and alert, Bubo stands up tall and clacks his bill as if he's in charge here. His fluffy down has dried, making him look twice as big as before. He spreads his wings and raises the feathers on his back, and he looks larger yet. Then he faces me and continues to clack his bill while rocking from side to side, missing no trick to make himself look as large and menacing as possible. All the while, his eyes do not leave me.

Bubo
as owlet

His large yellow eyes are positioned on the front of his flat face, not at the sides as with other birds; his eyelashes are very thick. I remember reading that baby great horned owls are born with pale blue eyes that change to yellow long before the owlet leaves the nest. Where one would expect a nose on a human face, Bubo has a curved bill with a nostril on each side. Most of the bill is hidden by stiff, hairlike feathers.

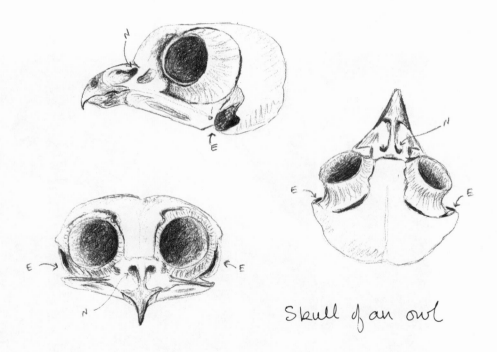

Skull of an owl

Bubo is only three to four weeks old. He already weighs about three pounds and will not gain much more weight. Young great horned owls achieve nearly their full weight but not their size by this age. I measure Bubo, and, standing flat on his feet, he is about twelve and a half inches tall. He may grow another seven inches or so by the time he is an adult. I am awed by the thought that his wingspan may grow to fifty-five inches! Right now he hardly extends his wings at all, and his feathers are still short: his tail is a mere stub, and his wing feathers extend less than an inch beyond the quills. But the talons are already well developed, and sharp. As if poking

Bubo's talons

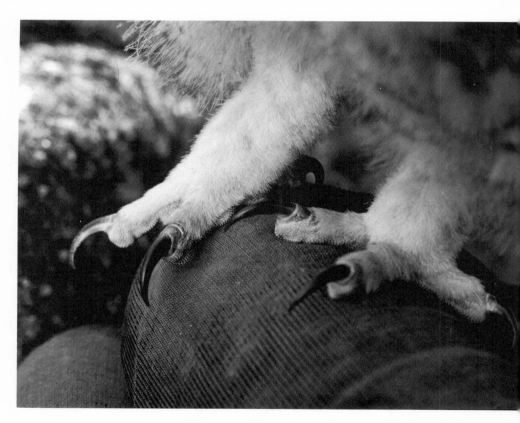

through wool socks, they extend ridiculously far beyond the ends of his toes, which are delicately covered in cream-colored down. Hanging over the legs and extending over both sides, the long, fluffy belly feathers look like a pair of bloomers.

His coat is functional: as long as it remains dry, it helps to keep his body warm. Owlets are covered with a fuzzy white natal down almost from the time they hatch. When they are about three weeks old, this down is replaced by a longer, buff-colored, soft and fluffy secondary down.

Though Bubo looks harmless and cuddly now, he will not always be that way. Great horned owls are known to be fierce, defiant, and untamable.

Bubo is now too old to be brooded, that is, his mother would no longer need to keep him warm with her body if he were in the wild. But as substitute parent, I still have certain chores. And he is not cooperating. He is standing at eye level in his cardboard box in front me, and whenever I move, he immediately hunches down, spreads his wings, and puffs himself out, rocking furiously from side to side. He hisses and snaps his bill in a rapid series of clacks. His suspicious, gleaming eyes stay fully open and follow my every movement.

In the evening, I cut up a dead mouse from the mousetrap and put a small piece into his hooked open bill. He clamps down on it, hesitates a second, and then swallows. No matter how gently I withdraw my hand, he is on full alert again and takes on a defensive posture with blazing eyes and snapping bill. Again I place a small piece of meat in his bill and speak to him softly, and the wild look in his eyes disappears.

Bubo as an owlet

April 24

After four days of being constantly at my side, Bubo is calmer. After I talk to him in gentle, soothing tones for about two minutes, he begins to smooth his feathers, closes his bill, and pulls in his outstretched wings. But when I make any sudden movement, such as turning the page of a book or lifting a pencil, he comes to full attention and acts as wild as before. So I talk to him again in a lulling whisper, and he calmly closes his eyes.

Bubo with outstretched wings

April 26

Bubo has been here for five days now, and he has become downright tolerant of me. By moving my hand very slowly, I can even reach behind him and scratch the back of his head. But that makes him shake his head, as if he is trying to get rid of a bothersome bug. I scratch there some more, and his feathers feel soft and fuzzy, warm to the touch. When I feel the feathers on his belly, he starts to groom his wings, drawing each feather through his big hooked bill. Then he proceeds to balance on one foot, closes his eyes, and gently scratches the feathers around his eyes with one of the great talons of the other foot. The preening completed, Bubo fluffs himself out and shakes himself violently. Finally, he rises tall on his woolly legs, stretches one wing and his neck, and gently sighs.

April 28

I want to transfer Bubo out of his nest box and onto the arm of the sofa beside me. This is not an easy task, because right now he doesn't want anyone to lay a hand on him. But there is a way. I put on a leather glove and place my hand under his breast. He climbs on, snaps his bill a few times, and clumsily shifts his weight from one foot to the other. Although this is the gentlest way of moving Bubo, I now have the problem of getting my hand back for other uses. It takes a bit of twisting to get him off. He moves around my hand like a lumberjack riding a log on a river drive. Soon he is perched beside me on the arm of the sofa, and, because he wears no diaper, I place a newspaper under him.

The time seems right for a meal, and I have just the thing for Bubo. Bunny, my wife Margaret's cat, has brought in a dead bird — a hermit thrush. I show it to the owlet, but he doesn't seem to recognize it as food. I wonder if his parents would still tear the prey apart for him. Would he accept the bird as food if it were cut up and handed to him in small pieces? I attend to this chore, and the answer to my question is a resounding "yes." After this meal, Bubo smacks his bill in contentment for two or three minutes, drawing his tongue in and out, in and out. He fluffs out and shakes himself, and seeing how snug and cozy he is, I feel happy, too.

After this ritual, he shifts his attention to his environment. Turning his head around ever so slowly — right, left, up, down — he inspects the walls, the floor, the ceiling; then he peers out the window for a while. Next, the wood stove becomes a big attraction, and he excitedly bobs his head up and down and to the side and back. This bobbing action helps him to gain depth perception, view an object from several directions, and get a clearer view of the stove. After a frenzied ten-minute inspection of the whole room, during which he totally ignores me, he makes a decision: he leaps off the sofa and onto the chair. His feet grasp the cloth of the chair, but his heavy body lags behind, so he dangles from a talon or two and weakly flaps his wings. I help him onto the

Bubo bobbing his head

chair and his talons draw a few drops of my blood. Then he bumbles onto the floor, and walks on his oversized feet by hunching down and leaning forward, taking slow, clumsy, purposeful steps while his wings are pulled in tightly. A ballerina he is not. Margaret does not like the floor whitewashed with Bubo's droppings, so I diligently return him to his perch over the newspaper.

May 4

Bubo is beginning to show some hunting instincts. Earlier today he carefully watched a large beetle scurry along the floor, although he did not attack it. Now he is playing hunter by attacking a leaf and a piece of straw from the broom, grasping them in one of his huge taloned feet. He lifts the foot up to his face, and with great care transfers the objects to his bill. He is amazingly persistent and undisturbed by my laughter.

How much will Bubo's natural behavior change because of his association with me? It is not likely that he will hunt like a "real" wild owl as long as he is watched by a human observer. But the instincts to hunt and fly are there within him, and, given the opportunity, he will learn to do both. I intend to make sure he gets that chance.

Owl at Kaflunk

Bubo needed to learn hunting and flying skills, so I decided to take him to my cabin in the Maine woods for the summer. There I wanted to try my best to teach him the facts of a wild owl's life.

Camp Kaflunk is nestled in a small clearing next to ledges atop Adams Hill. The clearing is surrounded by white pine, red spruce, and gray and white birch trees. The nearby forest consists of red and sugar maples and beech, and farther down is a swamp covered with rich sphagnum moss and bordered by white cedars and balsam firs.

The cabin measures about twelve by twenty feet. A wooden ladder leads up to a small loft. Under the loft I have placed a pile of sawed firewood and a bed. Rough shelves for books are on the wall. At the opposite end of the cabin is a cast-iron sink. My desk is in between, in front of a window and close to a small wood stove

Camp Kaflunk

and a low table. No houses or cabins are visible through the windows in any direction.

The trip from Vermont to Maine takes about four hours.

May 8

We are on our way to Maine. Bubo's cardboard nest is closed, and the box sits on the backseat of my Jeep. Packed around it are blankets, sleeping bags, groceries, books, papers, tools, scientific instruments, and all sorts of other things I need not only to survive in the woods for more than three months, but also to conduct my field research on bumblebees. Margaret will join us in a week or two.

Bubo and I arrive at the foot of the hill near Kaflunk in the early afternoon, and now I have to make nearly a dozen trips up and down the steep half-mile trail to bring up the supplies. During the first trip, I transport Bubo. He rides perched on my arm, his head swiveling this way and that. However, we don't get very far before he hops to the ground and starts to run. I chase after him and catch him, again and again. I learn that the higher I hold him up, the less often he jumps to the ground, and the more quickly we get to Kaflunk.

View of white birches from my desk

Bubo on woodpile, when he is older

After having the run of the cabin for a few minutes, Bubo stares long and hard at the top of the woodpile. The woodpile it is. He climbs to the top, then settles there and goes to sleep while I continue to make trips up and down the hill.

May 9

Last night Bubo retired to the top of the woodpile and went to sleep before dark. He did not move from his spot all night. In the early morning, as I make a fire and prepare breakfast, Bubo's gaze from the woodpile follows my every move. His head turns slowly as he watches me with apparent interest. He is still perched in exactly the same spot when I come back to the cabin in the evening to cook supper. He looks calm and drowsy.

About half an hour later, however, he becomes quite another owl. His head suddenly begins to swivel in all directions, and after a few mad hops around the wood he jumps down to the floor. He gives a little whisper of a hoot — "hooo-hoo-hoo-hooo-hoooo" — and then his head begins to turn in quick, jerky motions, first in one direction and then in the other. The head turns are so swift that, as with a propeller, the motion itself is barely visible.

Having explored the floor to his satisfaction, Bubo hops onto the bed, on which there are blankets, pillows, two jackets, and my running shoes. First he attacks and shakes the shoes, and then in turn the red jacket, the blanket, and finally the dark blue jacket.

Bubo is busy at this task for twenty minutes, and judging from the way he smacks his bill and moves

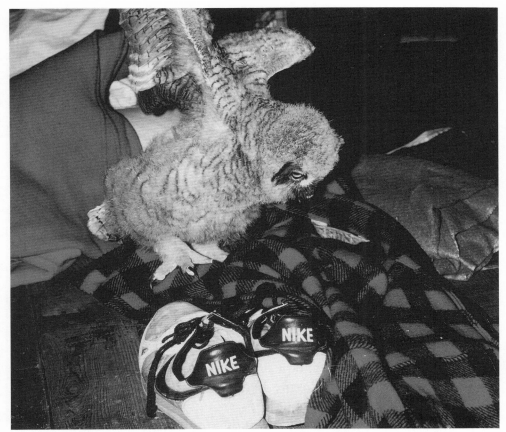

Bubo attacking shoes and jacket

around with such energy, he is enjoying himself greatly. I call him again and again and wave my arms to get his attention. Does he have even the slightest interest in me? No! Occasionally he will stop and look up. But almost immediately thereafter he continues to do what he had been doing, leaving me to wave my arms and shout myself hoarse.

Bubo is a born hunter, and he wastes no time trying out his skills. Any object is fair game. I decide to play with him to see what he can do and how he will react. I pick up a pencil and roll it across the floor. Will he chase the pencil as a form of play, or will he think it is food? It stops rolling, and Bubo stares at it for several seconds. Then, with his neck out- stretched, he scurries toward it and pounces. He picks it up with his right foot and tries to bite it. He nibbles on it, but it slips from his bill. It rolls on the slanted floor

Bubo playing with pencil

until it disappears out of sight under some shelves. Out of sight, out of mind? Not with Bubo! After a pause and another look around, he runs ungracefully but quickly to the shelves, trying to pry underneath them with his bill. Sorry, Bubo. There's no room for an owl's big head under there. I decide he is just playing and that at this point in his development he does not connect the chase with food.

After dark, Bubo executes one final attack on the jackets and shoes. Then he jumps up onto his woodpile, pulls his head down into his shoulders, blissfully smacks his bill, and slowly closes his eyes.

May 10

Bubo was quiet all night, and this morning he is standing in exactly the same spot where he went to sleep last night. He stays there all day, and now he is stretched out flat like a sleepy puppy, with his feet in front of him. His head is resting on his taloned feet, and his eyes are partially open, lazily watching me. Some bird.

Later, Bubo pumps his wings a bit and hops down onto the floor. Curious and suddenly excited, he pounces on a knot in the floorboard and then onto a little white speck that flew from his feathers. Then it's up onto the bed and another impressive inspection of the shoes and jackets.

May 11

I go into the woods very early in the morning to do some work. After returning to the cabin a few hours later to escape the freezing temperature and dreary drizzle, I am cheered by Bubo's companionship. He perches on my arm while I make myself a cup of coffee. When I sit down to read, he amuses himself by nibbling at the buttons on my shirt. But he doesn't nibble only on buttons. Whenever my hand comes near his bill, he nibbles on my fingers as well, and we play finger-bill games for about half an hour. Does he confuse my fingers with edible meat? To find out, I hand-feed him a mouse from the trap in the pantry. He eats eagerly until he is full. Then I offer him my bare finger, which he nibbles gently.

Bubo showing interest
in a spot on chair

He is indeed distinguishing between what the fingers
hold and what they *are*.

Within an hour, Bubo's appetite is back again. I still
wonder if he will eat whatever I give him, so I experiment a little further. I hold a piece of birch bark in front
of him. He grabs it — and gulps it down. But it doesn't
go far — he immediately regurgitates it. When he finds
bark anywhere else, he only plays with it, never swallows
it. Bubo, I am honored that you trust me so much that
you'd swallow birch bark for me!

It is now raining and sleeting hard, so I sit by the fire and read all morning. I remove one log after another from under Bubo and place them into the fire. He has a hard time settling down, being disturbed so often by having his perches removed from under him. He finally comes to rest on top of a thick log, but his head droops down over the side, and he looks uncomfortable. I decide that he needs a proper bed.

A shallow cardboard box filled with dry leaves and pine needles and placed on top of the logs does nicely for a nest. Once inside, Bubo shifts his weight on his feet and grabs a dry, wrinkled leaf in the steel blue talons of his right foot. The four talons lock inward in a strong

Bubo watching
a grasshopper

grip on the fragile, crackling leaf. He lifts the foot and looks at the leaf with interest, and then he nibbles at it. After a quick shake of the head, he drops the leaf, lies down again, and closes his eyes.

Later, I take Bubo onto my arm and scratch his head so that I can observe the details of his expressions. When he is at rest and at peace, the feathers above his bill rise and make his face appear fluffed out. He partially lowers the top lids and slightly raises the lower ones, and his eyes take on an oval shape. Occasionally, one eye remains open while the other is closed. But when he is at full attention, both eyes are wide open and the feathers of his head are pulled back, making his eyes appear large and round.

May 13

Bubo is greatly excited as I take him out for a walk on my arm. In no time at all he hops onto the ground and runs into the woods. He pays no attention to me when I try to call him back, and I must follow him through the underbrush.

It is probably not wise to let him run loose yet. He is a long way from being a hunter, and I cannot predict where he might run off to. Even though Bubo cannot fly yet, I decide that, for the time being, he must be caged for his own safety. And so I build an aviary next to the southern end of the cabin. It measures about seven feet in height, is seven feet wide, and fourteen feet long. There is a window between the cage and the cabin, through which I can let Bubo in and out. The aviary contains branches for perches, and under one end, under the roof, I have built a large nest of sticks lined with grass and dried fern. What more could an owl want?

May 14

After I put Bubo into the new enclosure, he hops from branch to branch, and almost immediately heads for the nest. He relaxes there and then sleeps all day. So far, so good. He becomes alert at dusk, as usual, but spends most of the time gazing out into the woods. He spends the rest of the night on a perch, and whenever I look out from my bed to check on him, I see that he is wide awake, staring into the night.

Having Bubo caged is no joy at all. An owl is a part of the woods, and his instincts must be telling him that's where he should be. But I also know that he is not yet ready to fend for himself.

Bubo at night

Beginning Hunter

May 15

Last night Margaret and Bunny the cat arrived. When Bubo saw Bunny, he lowered his head and ballooned out to bushel-basket size by spreading his wings and raising the feathers on his back. Then he blinked and rocked slowly from side to side. Bunny meowed, pretended to be uninterested in the display intended for him, and quietly slipped out of the cabin.

In the morning I allow Bubo to come in through the window to keep us company. He eats a shrew and a mouse that Bunny has caught during the night, and he finishes his Sunday brunch by swallowing a chicken drumstick, which slips easily down his throat. The bone will not be digested. It will emerge intact inside a pellet within a day. Because Bubo does not cause much commotion during the day, we let him return to his favorite perch inside on the woodpile.

Bubo's eyes

When Bubo sits up there on the wood, at my eye level, I notice his eyes a lot. He blinks the same way we do, by moving his top lid down across the eye. But when he closes his eyes to snooze, he moves his bottom lids up. Both lids are feathered. He also has a pair of milky white inner lids called the nictitating membranes. They slide over the bright yellow eyeball as they are drawn from the upper inside corner diagonally across and down.

May 17

Cats are supposed to catch mice and remove them from the house, but Bunny catches them outside and brings them *in,* sometimes in a very lively condition.

Bubo with a deermouse

He brings us other wildlife as well, all of which is a boon for feeding Bubo. A favorite is the tiny smoky shrew, which looks similar to a mouse. Bunny deposits everything under our bed.

I supplement Bubo's diet with roadkills that I find as I jog along the highway bordering the forest. But Bubo, like all wild animals, must learn to hunt for himself. And it is my duty to teach him, so he can return to the wild and survive there.

In Bubo's first hunting lesson, I want to teach him to pursue prey. I tie one of the many available shrews onto a string and drag it across the floor. Bubo, perched on my wrist, comes to attention. He pounces and lands on the shrew. Then he brings one foot up to his bill to bite into his prize. But . . . what? Nothing? Bubo brought up the wrong foot. The shrew is under the *other* foot. I tug on the string attached to the shrew, making the small

Bunny the hunter

animal "escape." Bubo looks at it suspiciously and pounces on it again. Then he nibbles at it, loses interest, and drops it.

May 18

Whenever we open the window that leads to Bubo's cage, he knows it is an invitation to come inside. He does not yet have the power to fly upward, but he can proceed horizontally with ease for at least ten feet or so. Still, he goes most places on foot.

He hops up onto the top of the woodpile and lies down on an old shirt I have left there. With eyes half closed, fully closed, or sometimes fully open, he nibbles on the shirt or on his toes, while putting his weight on his "heels" so that his toes are raised. Occasionally, he stands and yanks vigorously at the shirt. Or he stands on one leg only, lifting the other one and nibbling on his talons. When a fly comes by, he stops his manual exercises, opens his eyes wide, and watches it as it circles him at a dizzying speed. Bubo moves his head in lightning-quick jerks to keep up with the fly's movement. But he tires of the quick action and fixes his eyes on a bird perched in the tree outside.

May 19

I make a fire in the stove, and after the stove is hot, an unsuspecting Bubo jumps onto it. He dances up and down, as though someone is shooting bullets at his feet, beating his wings and snapping his bill furiously. I think he won't try that again.

In the evening he is as active as ever, maybe even more so, because now he has discovered a wonderful new way of getting around: flying. Papers, dishes — nothing is safe from his mighty flapping wings. Good thing Kaflunk is not a china shop.

Bubo pouncing

I have saved a rabbit's foot from one of Bunny's "gifts" to us. I decide to use it in another training workshop to develop Bubo's hunting skills. I tie a string to it and pull it along the floor. Bubo watches alertly. He teeters after it, then pounces with his feet extended forward and his head back, in the classic pounce of owls in the wild. Only one problem: he lands a few inches short of the mark. No matter. He has another go at it and picks up the rabbit's foot in his bill and proceeds to swallow it. His first catch! The string trails from the side of his bill like a rat's tail. It seems that he understands now that he must chase to obtain food.

May 20

Bubo's back feathers are now well developed, but they are still fringed on the ends with tiny grayish white tassels of down. These tassels, which are the remains of his baby plumage, are starting to wear off, leaving the cream-colored feathers underneath. His breast and head feathers are still the off-white nestling down of three weeks ago. Apparently there is no need to shed them quickly. His primary feathers are almost full-length, and he is already growing entirely new chocolate brown wing coverts, which are the feathers that cover the base of the quills.

His legs are enclosed in a layer of fluffy, cream-colored feathers that extend all the way down and over the tops of his toes. The undersides of his toes have huge bumps studded with a dense covering of hard pegs that help him grip more tightly. His talons are sharply curved, and any prey that attempts to pull away will

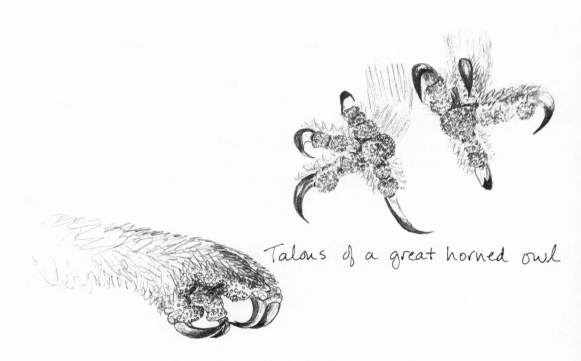

Talons of a great horned owl

impale itself even more as it tries to escape. But right now Bubo probably doesn't know his own strength, and it will be some time before he will use his feet as lethal weapons. For now he uses his talons to delicately scratch himself, or to pick up objects to bring to his bill.

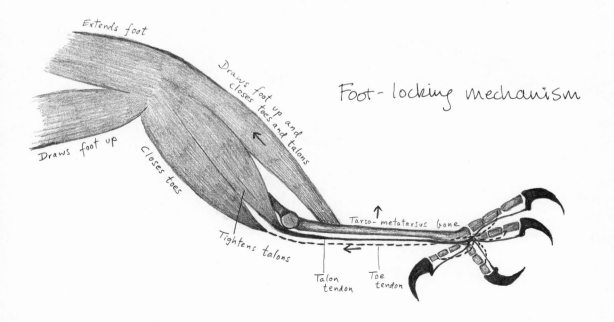

Extends foot

Draws foot up and
closes toes and talons

Foot-locking mechanism

Draws foot up

Closes toes

Tightens talons

Tarso-metatarsus bone

Talon tendon

Toe tendon

There is something unique about Bubo's wing feathers. They are covered with a soft, creamy down, and the small vanes jutting off the leading flight-feather shafts are curled, so that the edge of the feather is not sharp, as it is in most birds. This kind of feather construction makes flight less noisy, so that it is harder for the prey to hear the approaching owl, and also so that the owl hears less noise when trying to locate prey by sound.

Feathers of owls and hawks

Goshawk

I admire Bubo's thickly feathered feet and legs as he perches on my hand. Songbirds, which catch their food with their beaks and use their feet strictly for perching, do not have feathered feet. Why *does* Bubo have such thick stockings? From the point of view of warmth, it makes sense, because he hunts in the cold northern winter by sitting quietly in freezing weather for days. His feet must be quick and strong at all times, ready to catch prey at any moment, and the cold would make them weak and uncoordinated, the way my fingers get when I'm out in the cold without gloves. The stockings are also there for protection against the bites of prey. His thick down "skirt," into which he tucks at least one foot while he perches, no doubt helps to keep his legs and feet warm as well.

May 22

Bubo's wing exercises are becoming more vigorous every day. This morning I count six exercise bouts in all. Each lasts for several seconds and is repeated about every half an hour. He beats his wings three times per second — not bad for an owl with a four-foot wingspread!

May 23

Bubo hops onto the bed where Bunny is napping and stands up tall and stares at him. The cat stares back, and a staring contest begins. Who will back down first? The cat just lies there, acting bored as usual, but after a while he shows some nervousness by twitching his tail at short

Bubo with his eyes closed as he eats

intervals. Bubo continues to stare. After another half minute, Bunny becomes uneasy and suddenly bolts from the bed and sprints out the door.

Last night Bunny brought back another dead young rabbit. Though I am angry at him for his hunting successes, I am grateful that he provides meals for Bubo and there is no need for me to do so. As I give Bubo the rabbit, he begins to chitter excitedly, and with his eyes closed he nibbles all over it. He always closes his eyes when he puts his bill near food or prey. Is this an adaptation that prevents possible eye injury caused by struggling prey? After he has gone over the whole rabbit with his bill and massaged it with his toes, he drags it into the darkness under the bed. There I hear him take serious interest in his meal. He eats most of it, and pushes the rest into the farthest, darkest corner under the bed, where he has never dared to go before. Then he comes running out.

Bubo seems to know that being confined under the bed could be dangerous. When he sees Bunny strut by, he takes on a defensive posture and clacks loudly. At other times, when he is perched in an open area, he does not pay much attention to the cat. Is he able to visualize the potential danger of a situation?

I'm getting very fond of this bird, more than I could have imagined when I first picked him up with the idea of releasing him into the wild when he is ready. Will *I* be ready? Should I allow him out of his cage now, so he can try his wings and taste the freedom of the outdoors? Would he fly far away before I had a chance to teach him to become an efficient hunter who can survive in the wilderness on his own?

Freedom

❧∿❧

May 24

The cabin has always been crowded, and now it seems to be getting even more so as Bubo becomes more active. I have decided to give him his freedom because he is too confined here. Whether or not he stays will be up to him.

The door is open. Bubo walks to the threshold, bobs his head excitedly as he surveys his larger environment, and hops down into the grass. Not even the dead rabbit I hold in front of him distracts him. Instead, he flies from the ground straight up onto the roof of the cabin, and there he stays perched all day. Occasionally, he walks or flies back and forth along the ridgepole. After a while, I no longer worry that he will try to make a quick escape to far-off places.

A heavy rain drums on the roof. Bubo becomes soaked in minutes, and he pulls his wings in close to his body. The downpour continues all night.

May 25

Bubo flying

Bubo is still perched on the ridgepole this morning. He looks a bit bedraggled. His normally fluffy head and breast feathers are matted together in wavy strands, and after he shakes his head he has a tufty, ragged look about him. I try to tempt him back down by waving the rabbit at him several times, but he looks at me with no interest. Finally, in the evening, he launches himself from the roof, and in a graceful swoop lands about ten feet from me on the ground. He waddles forward and I give him the rabbit. His appetite is good.

After his meal, Bubo resumes his perch on the roof, and then he flies to the large white birch in front of the cabin window by my desk. I guess he does not yet care to go exploring. Instead, he sits, eyes closed, facing the evening sun.

May 28

It has been raining for two days and nights, but when we wake up at 7:00 A.M. the rain has stopped. The birds are active again outside and forage in the branches of the birch tree all around Bubo. The tree is still leafless, so the birds must see him. But they ignore him. And I had thought that birds always mob owls. I was wrong.

June 1

Over the last two days, Bubo has established a routine. It is simple: he sleeps on the roof, hops down to the ground in the morning to be fed, flies back onto the roof, and then flies to the large limb of the birch that faces the front of the cabin. He also has a newly discovered toy — the remains of an old anthill that is overgrown with moss. He plays with it after being fed and before flying back onto the roof.

Today he attacks the moss hummock with an energy I have never observed in him before. In his haste, he tumbles over onto his side, and sometimes he even rolls around onto his back. He strikes at it again and again with his powerful talons, driving them deeply into the green softness, tearing out tufts of moss with his bill and both feet. Occasionally he will stop and look around, and then he repeats his attack on the imaginary vicious thing. No doubt this activity sharpens the use of his legs, wings, talons, and bill, necessary for his survival later. This hummock, unlike prey, does not fight back at all, so all of his assaults are successful. And with Bubo, nothing succeeds like success. But how would he fare against *real* prey?

June 6

Even though Bubo has now enlarged his world to include the surrounding trees, he continues to stay quite close to the cabin. I need not have been afraid that he would get lost in the woods. If I can't see him, I call him by name, whereupon he wheels gracefully into the clearing in front of Kaflunk. It is a beautiful sight. Often he lands on the rocky ledges where he plays with me, and then stretches out like a cat to rest in the sunshine.

Sometimes, when he is being playful, he grasps my ear in his talons, and I cannot pull the offending foot away unless I want to risk getting my ears pierced. He plays rough, but so do I, and eventually he tires of it and lies down in my arms.

In the afternoon, my colleague Ken comes up for a visit. He is our first human visitor. Bubo eyes him suspiciously and seems nervous. Finally he comes to me, but keeps his distance from the stranger. After accepting a dead grouse from me, he makes a quick getaway into the woods.

June 7

This morning Bubo is not at all playful. Could he be upset about yesterday's visitor? Bubo can apparently tell people apart — he knew Ken was a stranger, and he always seems to know I'm me. Just to test him again, I put a pillowcase over my head to hide my face. I notice no change in his behavior.

June 8

I give Bubo his first road-killed snake today. I chop it into several sections, thinking that he might not know that a long thing that resembles a smooth rope is actually food. He eats every piece, and then I offer him a whole dead garter snake, which feels smooth and oily to the touch when rubbed in either direction.

Bubo picks the reptile up by the tail end and starts to gulp it down. After about five gulps, sixteen inches of snake has gone down into his crop, the pouch in his throat where food is prepared for digestion. Only a little over six inches to go. Then he seems to decide he has done it all wrong. He stretches his neck, opens his mouth wide, and out comes the snake, completely intact. He picks it up again, and this time Bubo does it the *proper* way: he starts at the head and finishes up with the tail, as is customary with owls. I would not have thought it mattered, really. But apparently owls have certain rules of etiquette.

So far Bubo has caught no live prey, but today he has made a start. He is perched on my wrist, idly biting the leather glove, when he suddenly perks up. Both of us hear a soft rustle close to the outside of the cabin. An investigation turns up a luna moth, fluttering in the raspberry bushes. Bubo watches it for about half a minute, hops down from my hand, and with one quick strike of his left foot he has it in his talons. Next he bites into it, making a crackling, crunching sound, and then he proceeds to swallow the huge, pale green moth in one gulp. He ends the meal with his bill-smacking noises of satisfaction.

June 9

This morning, under a bright and sunny sky, Bubo hops down to inspect the small pool of water that has settled in the rocks outside the cabin. He peers into the water, cautiously walks in, and dips his head down. He makes faint smacking-sucking noises as he brings his head up and swallows. As far as I know, this is the first

Bubo relaxing, with his wings down

time he has ever taken a drink. I am sure that he doesn't really need to drink even now, since he gets the moisture he needs from the meat he eats.

He continues to wade deeper into the pool, slowly and cautiously, ruffling his feathers and softly flapping his wings. And then he takes the big plunge. After completely dunking his head, he thrashes his slightly outstretched wings so vigorously that the water foams and sprays in all directions. Again and again, he dunks his head completely underwater and beats his wings, churn-

ing the pool like an electric mixer. All the while, he makes squealing noises unlike any he has ever made before. When he finally walks out of the water, he is completely soaked, and water runs in tiny streams off his matted breast feathers. He repeats the whole performance three times: his first bath is a thorough one. Then he flies up to the cabin roof and sits in the sun on one leg, with his wings drooping down. After an hour or two of playful preening, he is restored to his former, fluffy self.

Bubo bathing in the rock pool

June 10

This morning Bubo is high-spirited and ready to play. He nibbles at Margaret's shoes as she is sitting on the moss in the sunshine. When she gets up to leave, he chases after her, playfully pouncing on her moving feet. A moment later, I see that he has made off with the leather glove she was carrying. She catches up with him, tugs at the glove, and then I hear a scream. Clutching the glove, she runs back to show me the blood Bubo has accidentally drawn from her fingers. We are learning that to play with a great horned owl is no delicate matter. We must be cautious.

In the afternoon, I have a treat for Bubo — a dead red squirrel I found on the road. I hold it up for him to see, and he leaves his moss hummock and comes to me on the run. He enthusiastically grabs the squirrel in his talons and proceeds to squeeze it, as if trying to kill it. In the wild, an owl would rarely take a dead animal, and perhaps that's why Bubo treats it as if it were still alive. I have the squirrel on a fish line and yank it away from him. He gives it a brief, puzzled look and then pounces on it again. We play this game several times, and I am encouraged that Bubo is so interested in chasing his "prey."

Bubo plays with us much more aggressively now than when he was a younger, flightless owlet. He often flies out of nowhere to pounce on our feet or land on a shoulder, where he is likely to start tugging on an ear. He never bites down hard, so this is usually not a problem. But he holds on very tightly with his talons when he is excited, and it's impossible then to brush him away. So, we try to be very calm and cooperative with Bubo to avoid any dangerous entanglements.

June 12

The lazy little stream in the valley half a mile down from Kaflunk is well stocked with clams and minnows. I collect some of the clams and carry them back to the cabin. I crack one open and offer Bubo the contents. He holds the slimy mollusk in his bill somewhat reluctantly, and finally swallows it. I offer him a second one, but he looks at it with displeasure and refuses. Then I have an idea. Margaret has just finished brushing Bunny and is holding a ball of fur. I wrap the clam in the fur, offer it to Bubo again, and he swallows it with gusto. Apparently texture is more important to him than taste.

June 13

I sit down near the rock pool outside the cabin, and after I call Bubo he walks over and stops in front of me. He does not look up at me but down into the water. Strange — what could he be watching there? I look into the pool, too, and I find myself looking into his eyes through the reflection. He sees me in the water, too. But now he looks up and sees me *out* of the water as well. What's going on here? There's supposed to be only one man there! He jumps up and hastily retreats into the woods.

Bubo and his reflection in the rock pool

In a few minutes he is back again to check "us" out. He shows a shy respect for the water, but loses interest and flies onto a nearby stump. From there he suddenly pounces onto his moss hummock like a maniac. He pounds one foot into it, then the other, with all the force he can muster — one, two, three — harder, harder, harder. Then he bites into it with fury, yanking up tufts of moss with his bill.

Within a minute he is completely transformed again. He returns to the stump and calmly studies me for about ten minutes, as if he is hatching up a plan. Suddenly he launches himself over to the spot where I'm sitting, and with his left foot he hooks my shirttail while trying to hop away on the right foot. Alas, he quickly comes to the end of the shirttail, but the yanking continues. He is determined to make off with it, but nothing gives. So he adds a dose of wing power, beating his wings fiercely and continuing the big pull. Still no progress. He becomes irritated, making the loud chirring noises that indicate he is very angry indeed. A change of strategy is in order: he releases the shirt from his foot, turns around, and begins to pull it fiercely with his bill, bracing himself backward on both heels. More irritated chirring. Now he adds backward-stroking wing beats as well, but the shirt won't give. Well, Bubo, there are some things you just can't do, no matter how hard you try.

June 16

Bubo watches me as I come jogging up the path carrying, as usual, a plastic bag with roadkills. (Because I jog so much along the well-traveled roads bordering the forest, I unfortunately see just how many animals are killed on the roads. This happens mostly at dusk and in the early morning, when most animals go out to forage and all too often find themselves crossing a busy road.) In an instant, Bubo is next to me, and I shake a rotting bird from the bag. Despite its foul smell, Bubo grabs it and flies off to a stump under the large spruce. An hour and a half later, I see he is still there, clutching the bird and occasionally giving it a nibble. He has eaten very little of it and seems undecided what to do. Is he too greedy to let go of it, yet too nauseated by its decay to eat it?

Bubo watching me

Long after dark I hear something on the roof, and shining my flashlight up there, I see him on the ridgepole, with the rotten bird still in his clutches.

June 19

Until now, Bunny and I have been able to provide Bubo with all the food he needs — Bunny with his hunting exploits, and I with the small dead animals I find on the road. But the day was bound to come when neither of us would have anything to offer.

I must now make my first conscious decision to choose Bubo's life over that of another creature. Bubo watches me as I leave the clearing with my rifle. After I have walked for about five minutes, he suddenly makes an appearance, flying down through a hole in the canopy of spruces. He lands beside me, and as I continue to stalk "our" prey, Bubo follows me on foot.

On one of my stops to look and listen for red squirrels, I notice that Bubo is no longer behind me. I hear a squirrel chirring nearby, and I go to investigate. Bubo is already there, watching the little red bundle chucking and scolding up in a spruce tree. He watches the rodent with interest, but does not give chase. I am a little disappointed in him, for now I have to shoot it myself.

But my shot is not good. The squirrel tumbles to the ground, merely wounded. As I worry that it might escape and suffer needlessly, Bubo dives through the branches, breaking and scattering twigs in his haste as the squirrel tries to scamper away. In seconds, the squirrel is securely in Bubo's talons, and I stand there amazed that he knew exactly what to do and when to do it.

For the next ten minutes, Bubo subjects the squirrel to the sharp spikes of his toes, which have now indeed become lethal weapons. He bites into it repeatedly, starting at the head, then eats half of it and saves the remainder for later by hiding it under a small fir tree.

June 27

This morning Bubo seems more hungry than usual. For about two weeks now, his begging noises have sounded like blasts of escaping steam. There is only one way to shut him up: give him food. Today it requires a warbler, a mouse, half a young rabbit, and one automobile-flattened young ruffed grouse. I wonder if parent owls react like I do, frantically searching for food to stop all the racket.

July 1

As evening approaches, Bubo sits in front of the cabin, looking in through the window. His begging calls are constant and annoying, but I'm trying to ignore them. If he is not allowed to go hungry, he might never be motivated to hunt on his own. Finally, I throw out a banana peel to pacify him. He pounces on it and tears it to shreds, shaking his head in disgust. He doesn't eat any of it.

So I go to a local pond. Perhaps some of the resident amphibians could be of help in sharpening Bubo's hunting skills. I call five unwilling bullfrogs into service.

I release one of them. Bubo stares at it and makes one hop toward it, as the frog makes one hop backward. Bubo's next hop, however, is right on target. He crunches the frog with his bill, though he shows a certain lack of enthusiasm for this meal. Whereas it takes him just one gulp to down his favorite foods, this one takes fifteen minutes to consume. I am reminded of a child being forced to eat spinach.

July 2

Bubo is even more hungry today, and I have some time to experiment with his taste in foods. I offer him a fresh bullfrog again, but he drops it immediately. So I take the skin of a red squirrel and put a bullfrog inside it. He recognizes the squirrel from its fur and joyfully grabs it from my hand, loudly chirring his enthusiasm. He even defends his meal with loud bill-snapping when I get close to him. He pulls out the frog meat, tears it up, and eats it with gusto. Apparently he likes the frog meat not on the basis of what it tastes like, but on the basis of what he has been led to believe it is.

July 3

It is raining. During a long rain, Bubo usually sits quietly, pulling his wings in tightly against his body like an overcoat. Not bothered at all by the rain, he perches out in the open, fluffs out his feathers, and opens his wings wide, shaking them while hopping around in great excitement. He is either taking a shower or doing a fair rendition of a rain dance.

July 11

Bubo's breast feathers are about halfway grown in now, and two dark shoots are sprouting through the fuzz on each side of the top of his head. They are the first hint of the "horns" or "ears" that will identify him as an adult. Each horn will eventually consist of about a dozen black-tipped feathers. His wing coverts are now smooth and shiny. They overlap one another like shingles on a roof and produce a silky surface that is almost water-proof.

Bubo is becoming quite a sight to see. It gives me a thrill to see the big bird come flying gracefully over the birches, wheeling down into the clearing and landing beside me when I call him.

First appearance of horns

July 16

This morning, while he is perched on my hand, Bubo hoots for the first time since he made those tiny whispers when he was still a nestling. I answer him, he answers back, and we answer each other back and forth several times. Not only do we hunt together, we also sing together.

July 17

We have begun building a log cabin in the clearing by the old farm site below Kaflunk. Bubo comes often to investigate. He uses the framework of the cabin for his various perches. Does he also come just to be with us, for company? In my selfish way, I hope so.

July 18–19

Bubo does not come around much these days. He comes once a day to get fed at Kaflunk and often makes a social call when Margaret and I are working on the log cabin.

It is a beautiful summer morning. After having been fed, Bubo takes a leap to the top of the open screen door so he can check out Bunny, who is below him on the threshold, taking a nap in the sun. Bunny wakes up and leaves to continue his nap elsewhere. Then Bubo, energized by the morning warmth, hops down to his

Bubo on his moss hummock

moss hummock. He stands there for a few minutes to survey his surroundings, acting like king of all hummocks. Then, all of a sudden, he strikes the moss with his talons at a most frenzied rate. The pace is more than he can manage, and he soon collapses on his side and gets entangled in a loose rope. But he continues his thrashing, tossing billfuls and fistfuls of moss in all directions. Then he pauses and quickly shifts his attention from the moss to the rope. He pounces first at one of its tangles with his right foot, and then at another with his left foot, flapping his wings in an attempt to keep his balance. Then, as suddenly as he began this assault, he launches himself quietly and gracefully and flies off into the woods.

July 23–25

Bubo seems to enjoy his freedom to explore the outdoors more and more. I meet him deep in the woods today, near the brook. He comes to greet me with a soft hoot, which to me is the same as a friendly handshake. He watches me walk up the path but does not follow. Even though I call him repeatedly, he does not appear at Kaflunk this evening.

Bubo is becoming independent, and I miss him when he is not around. But when he does come to beg for food, I don't know whether to accommodate him or to let him stay hungry. To be safe, I feed him, although it's likely that, in the wild, he would be on his own by now.

His ear tufts have grown almost to their full length, and Bubo now truly looks like a great horned owl.

Bubo in his adultlike plumage

A Good-bye

We have to leave Kaflunk soon to return home to Vermont, and I will have to make a painful decision about Bubo. I would like to leave him here, giving him the freedom of the wild. But I'm afraid that he will starve. Maybe I'm also afraid that I will miss him too much.

To find out how dependent he is on me for food, I have kept daily records of what I have given him. He refuses food only rarely, maybe when he has made an occasional kill on his own. But on the whole, he probably still depends on me, and he knows it takes less effort to find food at Kaflunk than in the woods. I may not have been harsh enough with him. Unlike songbirds, birds of prey can go without food for as long as a week, and I probably should have withheld food from Bubo for longer than I have been, to make him more willing to hunt. Now, because I care about him so much, I find it harder to take a risk about his well-being.

August 11

Early evening. I haven't seen Bubo for over a day. I go outside to call him, and within a minute after I return inside, I hear his familiar thump on the roof above the patter of the raindrops.

Now he is perched opposite my window in his big white birch. His left foot is completely pulled up and tucked into his sleek breast feathers. His head, tucked down into his shoulders, sprouts two long "ear" tufts that stick out to the sides. Slowly, very slowly, he rotates his head to the right, then to the left, as he peers at me idly through his half-closed eyes. He blinks one eye, then the other. Once in a while, he cocks his head to the side, rotates it a bit, thrusts it forward, and blinks both eyes. Then he bobs his head forward, and

Bubo with his long "ear" tufts

then back again, blinks the left eye, and bobs his head up and down. He turns his head horizontally, then vertically, blinks his right eye, closes the left eye, then both eyes, or leaves them half open. And so it goes steadily and calmly for at least an hour. Only one thing remains constant: his left foot stays up.

August 24

Our summer at Kaflunk is over, and it is now time to face our responsibilities to Bubo. If he had learned to hunt on his own, we could just leave him here. He might even still be at Kaflunk next year when we come back. But great horned owls have only about a fifty-fifty chance of surviving their first year, even when they have had a "normal" upbringing, and to me the odds are too risky.

I must now cope with the fact that Bubo is no longer just any owl to me. He has been tamed by me, and we have become very close: we have "bonded." I know that as far as nature is concerned, Bubo's life or death makes no difference. He is only one great horned owl among many, and not an endangered species. But to me, because I know him *personally,* his existence and well-being do matter.

My choices are to leave him here, cage him at home in Vermont, or take him to a raptor center that specializes in rehabilitating injured birds. Even though Bubo is not injured, I decide on the latter, because there he might really be taught to hunt and eventually be returned to the wild with a fair chance of surviving.

August 28

Having made the decision to transport Bubo from Kaflunk, I must now do so. I show him a piece of squirrel meat I have put in a large cardboard box lined with fir branches. Unsuspecting, he hops right in and I close the top. Though I expect him to put up a fight, he is as docile as a drowsy cat as I carry the box down the road to the car.

The lady in charge of the predatory birds at the raptor center loses no time in advising me of my error in taking Bubo from the wild. I am told sternly that I have been "messing" with nature. I know I have, and I feel properly chastened by her scolding. And so I remain silent.

She puts on a pair of thick, heavy welding gloves and rips open the cardboard box. Bubo looks up meekly. The big gloved hand reaches in and grabs him by the legs. Swinging upside down and beating his wings in vain, Bubo clacks his bill furiously and turns his head, looking around helplessly with his bulging yellow eyes.

The lady places Bubo into a roomy wire cage and slams the door shut behind him. Other cages near him hold a red-tailed hawk recovering from gunshot wounds, a number of other great horned owls, a Cooper's hawk with a missing wing, and a very sad-looking raven.

The plan is for Bubo to learn to catch mice released into the cage. If he becomes good at it, he will be offered rats, and then possibly graduate on to rabbits. I will receive a call in two or three weeks telling me whether Bubo can be rehabilitated.

September 16

The long-awaited call came today. The news isn't good. The verdict is that Bubo is not earning his black belt in prey catching. He doesn't even try to catch meek and slow laboratory mice released into his cage. I find this news very strange and puzzling. He had never balked even for an instant at Kaflunk when a mouse or other small animal was catchable. But now Bubo is pronounced "incorrigible."

I am told that he cannot be released into the wild because he will seek out humans and approach them for handouts. Few people would tolerate a huge beggar owl. They will mistrust his intentions and kill him, I am told.

Is Bubo now destined to spend the rest of his days between the one-winged hawk and the sad raven? Back in April, should I have let nature take its course?

Reestablishing Friendships

Bubo passed the fall and winter in his cage at the raptor center. I was told that he ignored everyone there, even those offering food. Six dead mice were left for him on a shelf every night. He waited until dark to retrieve them and eat them alone. Leather straps were put on each leg to hold him forcibly on someone's fist so that he could serve as a "demonstration owl" for the public. Bubo must have resisted fiercely — there surely were some heroic struggles! He no doubt hated all attempts at "rehabilitation."

If Bubo could not be rehabilitated, then I wanted him back, because I don't like to see animals institutionalized. The woman at the raptor center told me that Bubo had changed, that he is unfriendly and indifferent. But if I insisted on having him back, he would be returned to me in mid-May.

To prepare for his arrival, I built a large flight cage in my backyard in Vermont, complete with a roof to create a dark, shady nook. In the center of it was the large trunk of a pine tree, complete with limbs. Two poles served as additional perches.

May 19–23

Bubo is in his new cage by the garden. He is perched in the darkest corner and doesn't move an inch, and his huge, pale yellow eyes are always open.

Bubo, showing his new white Bib

His massive curved bill is partially hidden by a bushy mustache of bristly white feathers whose wiry ends look like they have been dipped in India ink. Directly under his bill, the feathers are almost horizontal, so it looks like he is wearing a ruffled collar around his throat. And just beneath this collar Bubo now has a large white bib surrounded by black-tipped feathers. He looks like a beautiful owl, all right — a lifeless, *stuffed* owl.

He doesn't recognize me when I enter the cage to talk to him, or else he no longer cares because I "betrayed" him. Instead of making the little grunts of contentment he used to make when near me, he now emits a faint, dull hiss. When I walk closer to him, he opens his bill a bit, showing that he is either afraid or not pleased. He chirrups angrily when I put my gloved hand near his feet in an attempt to lift him. I persist, and he sleeks back his feathers, takes on a very erect posture, and heads for the perch farthest away from me. He chitters again and pays no attention to my offerings of food.

I had hoped we would still be good friends, but I don't seem to matter to him at all.

May 24

For four days, every morning and every evening, I have been trying to tempt Bubo with pieces of muskrat and squirrel meat, but he pays no attention to these tasty morsels.

Today I have something new, and I hope more interesting, to offer him — two young mice, live ones. For now, so that it won't escape, I tie a string to the tail of one of them and put it in the cage. I don't really expect him to catch the critter, since I have already been told that he refuses to capture mice.

The mouse sniffles about on the dirt floor and shuffles around, with the string trailing behind. Bubo looks down from his perch, cocking his head first this way, then that. But then he loses interest and pulls his head down into his shoulders. His gaze shifts blankly into the distance.

Bubo upon the return
to his aviary in Vermont

Six days without food, and he still shows no interest in *a live mouse!* He acts as I've been told, but I don't give up on Bubo so easily.

Maybe Bubo will show more interest if the mouse is closer to him. I bring it up to the branch on which he is sitting. The mouse walks along cautiously and seems more concerned with the long way down than with the owl straight ahead. Bubo, meanwhile, cocks his head again and shows some interest as the mouse approaches his toes. He shifts his weight slightly from one foot to the other, as if he is uneasy and unsure about what to do if the mouse should come any closer. When the critter is finally next to him, Bubo very casually lifts his nearest foot and neatly plucks it from the limb. The tiny rodent squirms only briefly as the talons curl securely around it, and Bubo's foot lifts it up to his bill. The mouse hangs there limply for a few seconds and then gets dropped to the ground. Bubo glances down casually, then goes back into his trance.

Later in the evening I reenter the cage with mouse number two and release it on the ground. It scurries around for about twenty seconds, all the while watched by Bubo from above. And then — hurray! — Bubo drops from his perch and pounces on the mouse with both feet. After a brief look around, he flies back to his perch with the mouse in his talons, and in one gulp he swallows it.

May 26

Throughout the day, Bubo sits quietly on his perch. Only his eyes, which are always open, show any sign of life.

In the evening, he hops to a branch near the front of the cage. I take the opportunity to offer him a long-stemmed dandelion and push it through the wire. He reaches over, chitters in a whisper, and yanks out some of the petals while shaking his head in disgust. But he continues to pull out and scatter a few more petals anyway. Is he playing? Hungry? I offer him some squirrel meat. He holds it limply in his bill, then drops it. I offer it again. This time he flies to the ground with it and goes off to a corner of the cage, where he hides in the grass. He is still not hungry, but he seems to have a bit more zest for life.

1. Angry
2, 4, 5. sleepy
3. At ease
6. Curious

Bubo in his different moods

May 28

For over a week now I have talked to Bubo at least an hour every evening and again at dawn, the times when he is most alert. I think this attention is paying off, because now, instead of opening his bill and hissing when I approach, he bobs his head up and down and makes his little grunting sounds. When I hold my fingers near his bill, he closes his eyes and nibbles at them gently, and when I offer him my forearm, he nibbles at it as well.

When we return to Kaflunk for the summer, I hope he will perk up even more.

Return to Home Territory

֎

June 1

I am bathed by the warm light of the kerosene lamp, and I hear the wind rustling through the trees outside. From the distance, down off the ridge, I faintly hear frogs. No cars. No airplanes. No TV. No phone. It's good to be back at Kaflunk. Bubo and Bunny are with me, but Margaret is visiting her parents with our six-month-old baby, Stuart. They will join us soon.

Bubo is in good spirits after our ride from Vermont. He stopped struggling when I finally cornered him in his cage and placed him in the now-dreaded cardboard box. He is now in his old aviary next to the window. He comes to the window and cranes his neck to look inside the cabin, chuckling and bowing to me, plainly showing excitement and maybe even pleasure. He remembers! Whenever Bunny comes close to the window, Bubo ruffles his feathers, hisses, and clacks his bill. He even has the same distrust of Bunny as before.

June 2

I've been busy this morning unpacking and getting the cabin back in order. Bunny is sleeping on my bed next to the window. I open the window to the aviary. When Bubo hops onto the windowsill and stares at Bunny, the cat gets up, meows, and climbs the ladder to the loft in search of more private sleeping quarters.

Bubo, pleased with the removal of the offending animal, charges in and with a graceful swoop lands on the rafters. Then he sets out to explore the cabin, getting reacquainted with his old surroundings. He flies from rafter to rafter, rafter to floor, to the sink, woodpile, table, chairs, desk. The only place he avoids is the stove, maybe because he remembers his little surprise of a year ago. He shreds a roll of toilet paper, attacks the leather gloves, tears the washcloth into strips, pounces on a dead mouse, and, after swallowing the mouse, carries a T-shirt up to the rafters for future assault. He continues to poke around, paying no attention to me at all while I unpack, sweep the floor, and tidy up.

An hour later, having finished cabin inspection, he seems content and settles down on a rafter. His lower lids are drawn up over his eyes, but he slowly opens his left eye when I talk to him. His ear tufts are erect, and his breast feathers are fluffed out. Two toes of one foot stick out horizontally from under his belly feathers, while the other foot is hidden. Meanwhile, he is rocking very gently from side to side.

A dull-sounding plop suddenly interrupts my concentration. Bubo has regurgitated a pellet. It is bright green. Can it be? Yes. It is composed of moist, com-

Bubo on the rafters at Kaflunk

pacted washcloth. It was produced in one hour, which must be a record time! According to what I have read about owl digestion and pellets, I should not have seen that pellet for another nine to twenty-four hours.

The owl's diet consists of meat, which is easily digested but must be separated from indigestible bones, fur, and feathers. This separation takes place in a complicated series of steps in the digestive tract. The indigestible parts are passed up in the form of pellets, while the digestible parts are passed as feces.

In the afternoon, Bubo awakens with a start, and a few seconds later I hear a holler from the trail below the cabin. It is my student Jim and his wife, Paula. I invite them in and they are almost settled down when they are startled by a full-volume, resonant hoot of the great horned owl. Bubo has finally found his voice again — and how! He stares at Jim with scorn in his blazing eyes, and more hoots follow. With each blast, his white throat bib becomes inflated. His head feathers are sleeked back, and his "horns" and tail stand erect.

Last year Bubo had not hooted so scornfully at strangers, even when he hadn't been too pleased by their visits. But now his hoots express power, determination, and anger. He focuses on Jim and ignores Paula. But his anger is general, and he attacks my glove, and even my feet. Jim and Paula had planned to spend the night, but they become uneasy and leave.

As they walk down the trail, Bubo hops down from the rafters so he can watch them better from the window. He continues to hoot at full volume until they are well out of sight. Then he shakes himself, preens, and is silent and at ease once more. It seems that Bubo has just

Bubo being angry

succeeded in defending his home territory against intruders.

But now I wonder what will happen to my social life and, worse, what will happen when Margaret and Stuart arrive later this month. Margaret and Bubo already know each other from last year, but I worry how Bubo will react toward Stuart.

June 3

It is 5:30 A.M. Before Bubo came into my life, I usually started my day a little later. But thanks to him, I have already had my breakfast and am enjoying a second cup of coffee in front of a cozy fire in the wood stove. Up here on the hill in Maine, the mornings are still chilly.

All was quiet in Bubo's cage during the night. But at the first hint of dawn, he taps on the windowpane next to my head. He is very persistent, and when I open the window, he hops onto the sill and surveys the room for a few minutes. The coast is clear. Bunny is sound asleep on the bed, having retired after his nighttime hunt. Bubo launches himself across the cabin and lands on one of the beams.

Many large birds have difficulty taking off to fly. Not Bubo. He has long, strong legs, and he can easily push himself off the floor and land on a beam eight feet above his head. When you see him waddle clumsily along the floor, it is hard to imagine him carrying out this feat so effortlessly.

7:00 A.M. The sun is now shining brightly, but Bubo continues to be active. He finds a roll of fish line and works it into a frazzle. He hops from the floor up to the beam and back down again. He preens and shakes, explores some more, checks out this thing and that, and finally relaxes by peering out the window.

Bored, he focuses his attention on the cat. He lowers his head, spreads his wings, and, hoping for some action, hisses at Bunny, who is still sound asleep. He toddles toward the unsuspecting feline with his head close to the floor and his body rocking from side to side. Bunny awakens but does not budge. Bubo, annoyed that the cat considers him no threat, turns about and slowly trots around the floor. Each little step makes a clicking sound as his talons hit the pine boards.

When I return to the cabin later in the morning after a four-hour absence, Bubo is fluffed out and asleep on the rafters, and Bunny is fast asleep on the bed. They show the utmost respect for each other's privacy. But Bubo has not been altogether unoccupied while I was gone. My green washcloth is on my desk, torn into shreds. I look up at him and ask, "Booo-bo, did you do this?" He opens his eyes, looks at me, and, as if on cue, stretches his neck and opens his mouth. Out pops a large green pellet composed of a long, crumpled strip of green terry cloth and fragments of a crayfish I had given him earlier.

June 4–5

Bubo is getting friendlier by the day. When I return to the cabin after attending to chores outdoors, such as cutting down trees and chopping wood, he always greets me by coming down from his perch. He plays with paper, pounces on shoes, tears my shirts, shreds toilet paper, and generally keeps himself — and me — entertained with his mischievous ways. When I read at the table, he comes to me and nibbles at the pages and on my fingers. I use the occasion to scratch his head.

But I'm less tolerant early in the morning. He wakes me up at around four o'clock by hopping around from perch to perch and rattling his cage, asking to be let in. I open the window while half-asleep and return to bed. Through sleepy eyes in the murky light, I watch him consider all the possibilities for mischief from his perch on the windowsill. Suddenly he launches himself toward his target — my gray sweatshirt. Before I can act, he sweeps it off the floor and flies to the rafters, trailing the shirt in his talons. I hear a couple of rips and a plop, a tangle with my running shoes, an assault on the broom. As the broom bangs to the floor, he bolts and flies off to the rafters.

I know I'm too easygoing with Bubo, but what else can I do? I can't sit down and reason with him and tell him to be a good boy. And I can't just boot him out of the cabin into an unknown wilderness. These, then, are part of the consequences of my commitment to him and his well-being.

Later in the day, I'm in a playful mood, too, and I give Bubo another lesson in chasing prey. I saved the tail of the woodchuck he fed on last night. I tie a string to it and pull it along the floor. Bubo sees the opportunity for fun and runs after it at once. He runs faster and faster as I keep it just out of his reach, until he finally catches it in his bill. But I yank it away. Irritated, he chitters loudly but resumes his pursuit. Round and round the cabin he goes, taking short leaps into the air, pouncing and missing his target, and trying again. Finally, he pounces with his talons held forward and his head back and succeeds in his capture. He wastes no time in swallowing the tail.

June 6

A reporter is coming today to learn about my life in the woods with a great horned owl. I build a fire in the stove and put on some water for coffee. I've swept the floor, picked up the shreds of toilet paper, and wiped the bird droppings off the floor, chairs, and table. Even the dishes are in a neat pile. In short, the cabin is ship-shape and as ready for company as it will ever be. Bubo, meanwhile, is perched on the leather glove he has been attacking since 5:00 A.M. But now, at 11:00 A.M., he is beginning to look drowsy.

Alertness in birds, as in humans, depends on body temperature. Our body temperature, and that of the great horned owl, increases in the day and goes down at night. This cycle matches Bubo's behavior: he becomes active at sunrise, is semi-active during the day, and sleeps at night. This shows that great horned owls were originally day-active but are now adapting into nocturnal, or night-active, creatures.

Bubo does not stay drowsy for long. I am just settling back and admiring my housework when I hear footsteps outside and a cheery "Hello?" Bubo, of course, hears this too. Instantly, he cranes his head down to about the level of his toes in order to get a look out the window from his perch up on the rafters. The sight must impress him deeply: he suddenly drops the cherished glove.

The reporter, a man of about my age and build, is at the door. Bubo's body becomes horizontal, his tail is raised, the feathers on his head are sleeked back, and the ear tufts extend straight up. His eyes change from round to oval, and his white throat patch puffs out as he hoots at full volume. The reporter stops in his tracks, but I invite him in. Bubo is not so hospitable and flies frantically around the cabin, making a shambles of my housekeeping, and hooting all the while.

Then he rushes at the reporter. That does it. We go outside for the interview, and Bubo's hoots continue to be heard from inside the cabin, along with an occasional crash. I try to make light of the situation, but the reporter suggests we find a less distracting place to talk. So we take a walk in the woods.

A full three hours after the reporter has left, Bubo is still causing a commotion inside the cabin.

I put up a sign outside: Beware of Owl.

June 10

Again I'm ready for bed early. Not only does Bubo get me up early, but sometimes he won't even let me sleep at night. Last night he tapped on the window. I tried to ignore him, of course, but the tapping was repeated every two or three minutes and became louder and more insistent each time. I was afraid he might break the thin windowpane, so I let him in, thinking he would settle down on a rafter and we could both sleep.

And indeed, he settled peacefully on the chair next to my bed, and I jumped back under the covers and dozed off. Suddenly, though, I heard a loud "splat" and fast wing beats. A mysterious clank. A smooth swish. Rattling silverware. The soft thud of a roll of toilet paper. I tried to block out the noises — the damage didn't sound too serious yet. A long silence. Then "click, click, click . . ." as he pranced across the floor. Splat, Another flutter. Rip. Silence. Rip. I bolted up and took full notice. Bubo stood on the table; the beam of my flashlight caught him holding the remains of my favorite shirt. I vaulted out of bed and yanked it out from under him. He chittered angrily.

All was quiet for a few moments after I crashed back into bed. As I dozed off once more, the pitter-patter of

"Beware of Owl"

little toes along the floor did not sound reassuring. A flutter. A soft landing at the end of the bed, close to my exposed toes — too close. Enough! I jerked out of bed.

I fetched the leather glove and held it near Bubo's toes so he could hop on and I could maneuver him out the window. But I received no cooperation at all. He had been having too much fun to be kicked outside. He chittered angrily, and as the chittering picked up in volume, he sounded like an engine revving up. He snapped at the glove, applied his death grip to it, bit down hard, screamed, and then hopped off. I grabbed a chair and held him at bay like a lion tamer. He attacked the chair, then flew over it to the opposite end of the room. This brawl had become a contest, and I was determined to win. I finally maneuvered him out the window and slammed it shut, leaving behind a hissing, bill-snapping, biting, clawing fiend.

Bubo nibbling at my fingers

June 11

Like an alarm clock, Bubo wakes me at 4:30 A.M. by drumming on the window. He joins me for breakfast, sharing some of my pancakes. He likes them either with or without Maine maple syrup. He swallows a mouse for dessert, and finally hops onto the back of my chair. I reach back and scratch his head, while he nibbles at my fingers and makes his friendly grunts. After I have had enough of this morning session of touch-and-feel, I try to write, but Bubo keeps inserting himself between me and my pencil. He wants fingers to nibble on, and fingers he gets. I do not disagree with a great horned owl unless it is absolutely necessary.

I know Bubo so well now that he has become fairly predictable in his behavior. I don't always like his ways, but I try to tolerate enough to ensure our mutual well-being.

June 15

Bubo joins me for a walk in the woods after breakfast. We have gone only a little ways when I spot a nest up in a small pine. I tap the tree, and to my surprise four young blue jays clumsily fly out of the nest, beating their wings rapidly. Bubo wastes no time chasing after the nearest one, and as I go after the hopping, fluttering jay, trying to save it, Bubo charges past me and catches it like a pro. With the bird in his clutches, he wheels about, facing me with outstretched wings and loudly clacking his bill, as if he is trying to tell me to keep away, that this is his.

Bubo's quick reaction and skill surprise me. He has never gone after an adult jay, so he must have known instinctively that he has a better chance of catching a young, inexperienced bird than an older one.

In another instant, the parent jays begin to dive-bomb Bubo and scream and scold him with all their might. Every time he tries to move or turn his head, he is greeted with another attack. This goes on for several minutes, and then Bubo becomes annoyed and hisses at them angrily. Eventually he is able to depart for a quieter part of the woods. He is now exactly where the adult jays want him — away from the rest of the young.

Soon he flies out of the woods, trailing his jay in his talons. He continues on across the moss-covered ledges with their scattered trees and lands on a patch of rein-

Blue jays
mobbing Bubo

deer lichen. He drops his prize near a stunted spruce, examines it briefly, then picks it up again and waddles full speed ahead. He sees me and looks at me with suspicion, then shoves the bird beneath some evergreen branches.

Thinking that Bubo doesn't want the jay, I decide to retrieve it and save it for him for later. But as I approach the area, Bubo swooshes over my head from behind, coming close enough to ruffle my hair. He has never flown so close to my head before. He lands in front of me, sleeks his feathers back, and stares at me. He is trying to give me a message, but I'm not reading it. As I prepare to pick up the bird, Bubo swoops down close to my head again and lands on the ground. He runs at me, clacks his bill loudly, then hoots at full volume, stopping only to start tearing away at my pant legs. My heart pounds wildly at this totally unexpected fury, and I make a hasty run for cover, with him in close pursuit. He follows me only a short distance, then runs back to retrieve the jay and hide it elsewhere.

Friends and Foes

June 17

Late in the morning I hear Bubo hooting, then human voices. My nephew Charlie and his girlfriend, Jody, are coming up the path.

Bubo wastes no time in making them feel unwelcome. By defending his territory, he protects not only the food he has already hidden but also that which has not yet been captured. He greets Charlie with an attack on the shoes, and I cannot pry him loose even with a stick. But a bucketful of water does the job nicely. Bubo, now soggy and no doubt feeling unduly disciplined, retreats to his perch on the birch, peers into the cabin, and hoots continuously at the company, getting angrier by the second.

Two hours later, they want to leave, but every time they open the door, Bubo swoops down at them and forces them back inside. I finally decide that the only way they can ever get out is to take along something that Bubo fears somewhat: Bunny. And so they leave, with Charlie clutching Bunny, and Jody clutching Charlie, and Bubo in hot but not so close pursuit. After a while, Bunny, having been released by Charlie near the end of the path, comes trotting back to the cabin.

Hours later, Bubo is still looking down the trail by which the company had arrived and departed, and he hoots for hours on end, without interruption.

Tomorrow Margaret and Stuart will arrive, and now I'm anxious about Bubo's reaction. I hope he can be friends with *all* of us.

Bubo attacking Charlie and Jody

June 19–20

Margaret and Stuart have arrived, and Bubo greeted them with vigorous unfriendly hoots. I feel uneasy.

Crisis. We are confronted by Bubo as we walk down the trail to go into town to buy some food. He swoops down, lands in front of us, hoots in anger, and runs directly for Margaret's legs. I hold him off with a pine branch, and then he attacks *my* legs. With a great deal of effort, we manage to get safely down to the road and into the car.

When we return from town, we're relieved that Bubo is not at Kaflunk. But he soon arrives in a hooting frenzy and lands in the spruce. Margaret and Stuart escape unhurt into the cabin.

As I go down to the well to fetch some water, I think about the grim possibilities. What to do? Even as I head back for Kaflunk, Bubo comes charging at me in anger. Is he angry because I allowed others to trespass onto "our" territory? Does he expect me to keep this hill only for the two of us? I decide to act as if I'm ready to fight back at him, and the bluff works.

But Margaret is not confident about being able to outbluff Bubo. She feels he has the advantage of weapons and surprise. At least he seems to have no interest in Stuart, but Margaret wonders if she will have to stay inside the cabin all summer, hostage to an owl. I can only be hopeful that they will be able to make peace with each other, and that we can all spend the summer in harmony.

June 21

Bubo has not bothered Margaret for a few days, so maybe things are already improving. I am greatly relieved.

This morning he stays close to where he hid part of a squirrel last night. He hoots at a broad-winged hawk perched in one of the nearby maples, and the hawk screams back. I wonder why the hawk is staying around here. Did he see Bubo cache his squirrel yesterday? Bubo flies closer to the hawk, and after an exchange of screams and hoots, the hawk swooshes close over Bubo's head. That brings the hooting to an end, but the owl, now silent, makes a pass at the hawk. The birds continue to swoop back and forth at each other in silence. Bubo has been sideswiped by hawks before, but this is the first time he chases back. No doubt he is protecting his squirrel meat.

June 22

Bubo is upset with me, and probably also with Margaret (and the hawk?). He begins to hoot as soon as I come out of the cabin, even as I give him pieces of meat. He does not tolerate my stroking his feathers.

One reason Bubo attacks others might be because he is imprinted on me, and he attacks other people the same way he would attack other owls to defend his territory. (Imprinting is a learning mechanism that appears very early in life, whereby, for example, an animal thinks a caretaker of another species is its parent.) That makes me wonder if he can recognize his own kind, so I decide to conduct a little experiment. I don't happen

Bubo sitting on the ridgepole, waiting for me

to have another great horned owl handy, so I get what I think is the next best thing: a full-length mirror.

Bubo looks at himself in the mirror, clacks his bill briefly, and takes on a threatening posture. But within a minute, he peers around the top and sides of the mirror and behind it. And then he ignores it.

He probably wasn't fooled for long. Maybe he's smarter than the many other birds that attack their reflection in a mirror or window.

June 23

As Margaret and I walk across the field to do some more work on the log cabin, Bubo starts to hoot. He is sporting his mean look today, eyeing Margaret hatefully. As we approach the cabin, he flies down and settles himself directly on the door opening, hooting ever louder. Margaret gets the message. We continue on to the swimming hole instead.

In the afternoon I go to the cabin alone to visit Bubo, because I know he has been spending a lot of his time there. This time he hoots without coming down to stand guard at the door. And he makes some high-pitched clucking sounds that I have not heard before. He might still be angry at me, jealous, glad to see me, frightened, or some or all of these at the same time. In any case, he sounds confused. I pull out a dead robin, and his hoots and clucks change to friendly chuckles.

He flies down to me and I sit beside him as he plucks and eats. After he is finished, he stares directly at me for a full minute, and then he comes closer. I hold out my hand nervously. To my delight, he begins to nibble on my fingers, first a bit roughly and then more gently. He continues hooting all the while, even as I stroke his head feathers and he closes his eyes. So he is still disturbed. But in time his hoots become softer, until they are almost whispers. I play with him about an hour, and I feel we have made peace.

Evening. My other nephew, Chris, and his friend Jeff have arrived at Kaflunk for a visit. The teenagers have blankets and sleeping bags and plan to spend the night. They have heard of Bubo, of course, but they don't yet know much about him.

Bubo makes his usual evening appearance at Kaflunk soon after everyone is settled in and chatting around the table. Unlike other evenings, we hear hoots from the tall spruce: apparently Bubo knows we have company. He flies down to the birch and perches low to get a closer look through the front window, his head bobbing in excitement. Then he flies around to the back window and presses his head against the windowpane. As Jeff walks over for a better look, Bubo throws himself against the window with a crash, and Jeff jerks back in surprise. Bubo looks for another way to get inside. Round and round the cabin he flies, checking all the windows and doors for a place to enter. The hooting rises to an ear-splitting pitch.

Neither Jeff nor Chris is eager to be the first one out the door to set up their tent. I try to lure Bubo away with pieces of meat, but he takes no substitutes: he wants Jeff. As Jeff opens the door, Bubo lunges down at him and he trips back inside the cabin. In his shock, Jeff neglects to close the door, and Bubo barges in. Jeff

Bubo sitting in the spruce

thinks quickly and grabs the broom, beating Bubo back out the door.

Both boys laugh, but I can see they're really tense about the situation. They admit they may very well be defeated by this owl. They won't be able to camp near the cabin, nor would any of us be able to sleep inside with the constant hooting and banging going on outside. It's clear (and sad) that Chris and Jeff can't stay. Because it's already getting dark, they must leave soon or Bubo will have an even greater advantage over them.

Unfortunately but not surprisingly, Bunny is no longer around to serve as a ticket out the door. I suggest that the boys throw blankets around themselves and try to make it down the trail so that they can pitch their tent on the field by the road, well outside of Bubo's territory. They get ready for a charge out the door, but Bubo quickly advances on foot, swaggering closer and closer to show his annoyance with the situation. More nervous laughter. What next?

Bubo is now positioned in front of the door, knowing quite well that the enemy must exit from there sooner or later. We discuss other tactics. There might be one way to disarm him: throw a blanket over *him*. I go out with the blanket, and fortunately he pays no attention to me; he wants one of those enemies inside.

I quickly drop the blanket over Bubo, catching him by surprise. The blanket muffles his hoots and screams, but he thrashes around wildly, and bulges pop out in all directions. The boys seize the moment and bolt out the door and down the trail. Ten minutes later I release my grip on the blanket. Bubo unravels himself, pokes his head out, looks wildly in all directions — all without

Buboo on the door at Camp Kaflunk

missing a hoot. After he's calmed down, he fixes a long stare down the trail the boys have just descended. Since he doesn't *see* them leave, I'm surprised he knows they are no longer inside. I throw him a big chunk of meat as a bribe to stay around the cabin.

I jog down the trail to see how the boys are doing. They are about ready to set up their tent, relieved that they made a bloodless escape. But then we hear a hoot.

We look up and see Bubo heading in our direction. He lands on a large maple, eyeing Jeff without blinking an eyelash. He leaves the branch and swoops down to the ground, heading in Jeff's direction. Jeff quickly wraps himself in the blanket, but Bubo continues to stalk. Just before the expected attack, Jeff unfurls the blanket and throws it onto Bubo. A good move. The muffled hoots sound more and more threatening as the dancing dervish under the blanket tries to escape. The boys grab their gear and charge down the road to their car, just in the nick of time. I feel sorry that their visit was cut short. This is what happens when one releases a "tame" owl.

Until now I had thought Bubo was mean to Margaret. But compared to what just happened, he had been treating her pretty well. He no longer bothers Margaret at all, so maybe he's looking for new enemies.

June 27

Bubo and I proceed smoothly through the woods today. We accidentally flush some sparrows out of a ground nest. Bubo sees a young bird trying to escape, and he catches the prey and swallows it quickly. The parents' strong protests can't save their youngster once it has been discovered by a great horned owl.

I find a wood frog and call Bubo, who immediately comes flying through the forest and lands by my side. I release the frog in front of him, and he walks toward it with great interest. The frog responds by hopping around in random directions, and soon blends in with the dead leaves. Bubo is puzzled; he has no idea where the frog ended up. I grab the frog and release it a second

Bubo in the woods

time. This time Bubo pounces right on target and immediately consumes his meal. Do wood frogs really taste that much better than the bullfrogs he despised so much last year?

June 28

Bubo is, I think, catching food on his own now. When he comes to me, he doesn't always beg for food. But when I have something available, I give it to him anyway.

July 20

For the past three weeks, Bubo has continued to follow some of his routine at the cabin, but he has been going out into the woods more and more on his own, and for longer periods of time.

He has been absent for several days now, and I'm glad that he's becoming independent and hunting on his own. But I'm also glad to see him back today. He is perched on the wood-chopping block by the doorstep, making his low, contented grunts, and we keep each other company.

The End of Summer

July 28

There is already a hint of red on some of the maple trees in the swamp, and the field, filled with a large crop of grasshoppers, is becoming cloaked with bright yellow goldenrod. Field crickets call out every evening from underneath logs near the cabin. And from the woods on warm days, one hears the buzz-saw drone of the cicadas. The insects are making preparations for the winter as the end of the summer draws near. The birds, on the other hand, are strangely silent this time of year. Most have raised their broods, and they are now busy foraging and getting fat for the southward migration.

August 8

The new log cabin is almost finished. The windows are in, and next year we can begin sealing the cracks between the logs.

Bubo and I outdoors

It is a beautiful, warm, clear day, and Margaret, Stuart, and I go down to the swimming hole. The sunlight filters through the light green leaves of the maple trees, and they sparkle as you look up through them from below. Down at the stream, the dragonflies are hunting small insects above the calm water. Water striders dimple the surface, and small minnows swim in the shallows, nibbling at my toes as I wade through the fresh, cool water.

Bubo has not come around for several days, but now I hear a familiar hoot from inside the forest. Is it Bubo, or some other owl?

A few moments later, a big owl lands in a white birch by the side of the brook. It *is* Bubo! He peers down at us, hoots some more, hops down from the tree and into the water, and thrashes his wings, merrily splashing the water around. Sufficiently cooled off, he leaves the water, fluffs himself out in the sunshine on top of one of the small boulders, and begins to preen. Margaret and Stuart are close by, but he does not bother them.

Well refreshed, we go back up the trail to Kaflunk. Bubo does not follow but flies upstream. Back at the cabin, I hear a muffled hoot in the distance. I call out to Bubo repeatedly, but he does not come.

Tomorrow we go back home to Vermont. I will leave Bubo here for now, since he seems to have accepted living in the wild. But I plan to come back and check on him soon.

Always Free

Two weeks after we returned home to Vermont at the end of the summer, I came back to Maine to see how Bubo was doing. He came to greet me at the cabin after I called. I still was not confident that he could survive the harsh Maine winter, so I took him back to Vermont with me. He spent the winter in a huge outdoor aviary in my backyard, where I continued to provide him with food and live prey.

As soon as the snow melted the following spring, I brought Bubo back to Kaflunk and let him go free. During that summer, I came to Maine only occasionally, and Bubo would stop by to say his hellos, as if out of politeness. He did not beg and ate very little of what food I did offer him.

He was less aggressive toward visitors that summer, but he was more aggressive toward me when I came near food he had hidden. Perhaps he no longer felt there was a threat to his territory, yet he had developed very strong instincts to protect his food.

Courtesy of Camden Herald

Bubo (?) in Camden, Maine, 3½ years after I last saw him.

By the end of August, when I left Maine to return to Vermont, Bubo had failed to show up at all.

But that was as it should be. Bubo was at last ready to be on his own year-round. Even though I felt a great sense of loss at no longer having Bubo as part of my life, I also felt great satisfaction at having prepared him to be self-sufficient. Indeed, in March 1989, three and a half years after I had last seen Bubo, I received a report of a "tame" great horned owl that had rested on someone's porch in Camden, Maine. Could it have been Bubo?

Great Horned Owls

The great horned owl is one of the more common owls and the most widely distributed. It lives throughout the United States and Canada and in the wooded regions of Central and South America; its range spans from the timberline in arctic Canada and Alaska to the Strait of Magellan in southern Chile. Not all great horned owls live in forests. In deserts, for example, they find shelter in cliffs and rock crevices.

There are ten subspecies of the great horned owl. They differ somewhat in size and color, but all of them are large and have ear tufts and a white throat patch. Its general size statistics are: length, 16–24 inches; wingspan, 51–57 inches; weight, 3–4 pounds. The adult female is larger than the male. She incubates the eggs and guards the nest and therefore has the larger size. The male may be smaller for two reasons: (1) small size makes him more agile in the pursuit of prey, and (2) after the chicks leave the nest and the female ends her guard, her large size will enable her to hunt for prey that has not already been depleted by the male.

Even though the great horned owl is not as large as the snowy owl and great gray owl, it is much fiercer and stronger. It has awesome power in its beak and talons. This owl can rip the wings from a hawk as easily as some other owls remove the wings from a moth.

In the eastern United States, the great horned owl nests most commonly in nests formerly used by red-tailed hawks in white pines, or by crows or ravens, although it will also nest in hollow trees, if available. In Florida, it often nests in bald eagle nests, and in Texas and the western United States it most often nests in a rocky cave or on a ledge. In the prairie regions and in Colorado it sometimes even nests on the ground.

The great horned owl nests earlier than any other bird of prey. In New England the female lays her eggs in February, and sometimes as early as January. The eggs are incubated for about twenty-eight days. Clutch size (the number of eggs) varies from one to five. If a clutch is destroyed by freezing during bad weather, the female may lay a second or even a third clutch. The young remain in the nest for six to eight weeks, although they are unable to fly until they are nearly three months old. About half the young do not survive their first year, usually because of starvation. In captivity, however, they have been known to survive for close to thirty years.

In flight, this owl shows a great sense of power. Sometimes it will flap its wings slowly, but it can also beat them with amazing speed. After the bird first launches itself, its legs dangle, but soon they are drawn up and tucked firmly against the lower belly. When diving for prey, it will almost completely close its wings and will not reopen them until the last possible moment, thus achieving great speed and accuracy in its attack. Its soft plumage and fluted flight feathers allow it to fly in complete silence.

How to Keep a Nature Diary

⚜

You can keep a nature diary, or field notebook, of anything in your natural environment that is of interest to you — a pair of nesting birds, a squirrel, a deer that strays into your yard in the winter, a garden, a tree you have planted, your own pet, or even a baby brother or sister. But you should not take an animal *out* of the wild just so you can observe it and write about it.

You'll learn much about plants and animals if you observe them keenly, but you must be patient. Changes usually don't occur overnight. Later on, though, you'll be glad to have a record of something special that you once observed. Once you start to keep your record, you'll be surprised at the details you notice about your subject. And in the wild, you'll also notice the relationship between plants and animals and the importance of maintaining the animals' natural habitats.

Remember, too, that diaries don't need to be as long and detailed as the one you just read!

Here are some suggestions you can follow:

1. Keep your diary in a handy place, along with a pen or pencil, so that it's readily accessible when you get the urge to write, or when an important event occurs.
2. Jot things down any time of the day. It doesn't have to be at day's end. But include the date. Sometimes the time makes a good reference point as well.
3. Write down everything that is of interest to you now, or that you think may be of interest to you or someone else in the future.
4. Jot down your observations every day, if possible, and note any changes you see. If progress is very slow, you may wish to write only once a week or so. If there's no progress at all, maybe you better look for another subject to observe! Also write down what you think may happen in the future. It's all right if you turn out to be wrong. Maybe next time, after you have gotten to know your animal or plant better, you will be able to predict behavior or changes more accurately.
5. If you are feeding an animal, keep a record of what food is consumed, and the amount.
6. Make sketches if you can, or take photographs and paste them in, to help record your observations.

Baby Birds: The Problems
by Gale Lawrence

At the Birds of Vermont Museum, where I work as a volunteer, we receive a flood of phone calls every spring asking us what to do about baby birds. In May and June many species have already hatched and are being fed in their nests while they grow their feathers and learn to fly. Baby birds have a way of tumbling out of nests. What should you do if you find one?

The first thing you should do is take the baby bird back to the exact spot where it was found. Look carefully for a nest nearby. If you find the nest and it is accessible, put the bird gently back into the nest. Contrary to popular belief, parent birds will not reject a baby that has been handled by humans. If you do this, you have done the best you can for that particular little bird.

The next best thing you can do is tie a small box, such as a berry box, into the branches of a tree or shrub near where the bird was found, and place the baby bird into the box. That way the bird will be off the ground and safe from neighborhood cats and dogs.

The third best thing you can do is simply return the baby bird to the spot on the ground where it was found. Parent birds are used to their young falling out of nests, and they will attend to them on the ground. Even though the baby is more vulnerable there than in the nest or in the box, it still stands a better chance of surviving under its own parents' care.

If the baby bird is truly abandoned or orphaned, which you can learn only by watching it from a distance for an hour or more, you have a problem on your hands. You can leave it there to die a natural death, which might in fact be the most humane thing to do. Or you can take it and care for it yourself. But you must remember that you are making a substantial commitment. Even if you live up to your commitment and put in a lot of time and effort, there is a very good chance that the baby will not survive.

There are two major problems when trying to parent a baby bird: feeding it and preparing it for life in the wild. Before you can attend to these problems, however, you have the more immediate problem of dealing with a shocked and frightened bird. You should send someone to get a book on the care of wild young, and find a heating pad or hot-water bottle to keep the baby warm. Then you must think about food. The parents were probably feeding it mashed worms, caterpillars, insects, and other high-protein odds and ends found in the wild. You must try to duplicate this food right away. Then you will have to identify the species of bird so you can determine whether it is a seedeater or an insect eater.

Parent birds feed their babies about every ten or fifteen minutes from sunrise to sunset. They also feed them exactly what they need to keep their bowels regulated and their bodies growing properly. In addition, they keep the nest clean by removing the babies' excrement, which usually appears shortly after they've been fed.

In brief, between finding and preparing appropriate food, feeding, and cleaning up after meals, you're not going to have much time for anything else for a while. If you do manage to keep the young bird fed and growing, you will eventually face the problem of finding a place where it can practice flying. You cannot expect a bird to go from your kitchen into the wild with one swoop of the wings.

After the bird can fly, you will need to continue feeding and protecting it while it is adjusting to the outdoors. The young bird is now at a distinct disadvantage because it has been raised by you and not its wild parent. It does not know everything instinctively, and you cannot guarantee its survival after it leaves you.

If you think I'm trying to sound discouraging, you're right. All your efforts will probably result in failure. You might even cause a death that would not have occurred if you had left the bird where it was. Remember that even experienced veterinarians have very little success in raising wild animals.

Perhaps the most important thing we can learn from an encounter with a baby bird is an appreciation of the way wild things differ from human beings and domestic pets. Whereas puppies and kittens warm to human attention and become part of the family, wild birds rarely will. Attempting to make a pet out of a wild animal is a serious disservice to that animal — so serious, in fact, that there are federal laws against it. Wild animals must remain wild to survive.

(Gale Lawrence is a founding member of the Birds of Vermont Museum in Richmond, Vermont.)